MACROEconomics
In the News

Genevieve Briand[*]

Macroeconomics measures the level of activity taking place in an economy, and focuses on larger sectors of the economy, like government, households, business and international trade. It also addresses how the government budget, as well as fiscal and monetary policies, regulations and trade restrictions, affect economic outcomes.

As a teacher of Principles of Macroeconomics courses, I share tidbits of economics in the news with students. In doing so, I hope to spark enough interest in the course and get students in the habit of being critical of what they hear and read, by questioning the logic and morality of the arguments presented to them.

MACROEconomics In the News goes over topics in the order in which they are usually covered in Principles textbooks. For each topic, the brief overview, econ. in the news, references to videos and data sources are those that I have chosen to share with students. This work was not sponsored by my past or current employers.

---

[*] University of Idaho, College of Business & Economics and Northwest College WY, Business. Previously at: Johns Hopkins University, MS in Applied Economics program; Washington State University, School of Economic Sciences and Eastern Washington University, Economics Department.

Brief & Select Contents

Contents

1 Prices & Unemployment

1.1 Overview

The Consumer Price Index (CPI) measures the price level. It is on the U.S. Bureau of Labor Statistics (BLS) website (1) that you can find the Historical CPI for All Urban Consumers table (CPI-U) https://www.bls.gov/cpi/data.htm (2)* .

What is the average of the CPIs for years 1982-1984?

Unemployment and Employment Rates are also reported on the BLS website. They are measured monthly via surveys of U.S. households, called the Current Population Survey (CPS), https://www.bls.gov/cps/ (3).

Go to Table 3 of the April 2021 BLS report (4): **Which race/ethnicity group has the lowest unemployment rate?** ***

* From https://www.bls.gov/cpi/data.htm (2), go to the All Urban Consumers (Current Series) Tables and then the latest Historical CPI-U (PDF) file or from https://www.bls.gov/cpi/tables/supplemental-files/ (5) go directly to the latest Historical CPI-U (PDF) file.
** You should find that it is equal to 100. The average price for years 1982-1984 is the benchmark against which we compare other years' prices. Because of that, the CPI corresponding to the benchmark years (or "base-year") is always going to be equal to 100.
*** In 2019, Asians did: See pp. 16-18 (4). Annual averages were: 2.7% (Asian), 3.3% (White), 4.3% (Hispanic or Latino ethnicity), 6.1% (Black or African American). The most recent "Women in the labor force: a databook" report can be found at: bls.gov > HOME tab: A-Z Index menu item > Current Population Survey (CPS) > CPS Publications tab: Additional Publications menu item > CPS Reports and Summaries, Women in the Labor Force: A Databook (**Archives and more**) (6)

1.2   To-Do-List

- Sign in your online course.
- **Read your textbook chapter**. (required)
- **Complete your Graded Homework**. (required)

Recommended Mary J. McGlasson's Macroeconomics Module videos (optional) (7):
(Macro) Ep. 16: Inflation & Price Indexes (9:20) (8)
(Macro) Ep. 17: Real Income (5:24) (9)
(Macro) Ep. 18: Unemployment (2:51) (10)
(Macro) Ep. 19: Types of Unemployment (4:20) (11)

Recommended Marginal Revolution University (MRU) Principles of Macroeconomics videos (optional) (12):
Unemployment & Labor Force: Is Unemployment Undercounted? (5:18) (13)
Inflation & Qty Theory of Money: Zimbabwe & Hyperinflation (4:19) (14)
Inflation & Qty Theory of Money: Price Confusion & Money Illusion (5:04) (15)

1.3   Econ. In the News: Jobs Report

The U.S. Bureau of Labor Statistics (BLS) (1) releases a jobs report (16) to the public, monthly. It describes how much payroll employment and the unemployment rate have changed, as well as provides two charts we replicate.

Go to: https://www.bls.gov/news.release/pdf/empsit.pdf (16)*
Read the first paragraph about last month employment situation.
By how much did payroll employment and the unemployment rate change last month?

* You can find the latest jobs report (16) by going to: bls.gov > SUBJECTS:
Employment: National Employment Rate > CES Publications: News Releases.
Alternatively, go to: bls.gov > ECONOMIC RELEASES: Latest Releases > MAJOR
ECONOMIC INDICATORS: Employment Situation (PDF). (The archived reports can
be found by going to: bls.gov > ECONOMIC RELEASES: Archived News Releases >
Major Economic Indicators: Employment Situation.)

Go to https://fred.stlouisfed.org/series/UNRATE (17) (18), and
https://fred.stlouisfed.org/series/PAYEMS (Charts 1-1 and 1-2) (19)**
Mouse over line charts 1-1 and 1-2 to read what the unemployment rate and
the number of nonfarm employees were last month.
**Is what you read off charts 1-1 and 1-2 consistent with what the BLS reported
for last month employment situation?**
Chart 1-1. Unemployment Rate (UNRATE series, 1948-01-01 to 2024-07-01).
Monthly data.

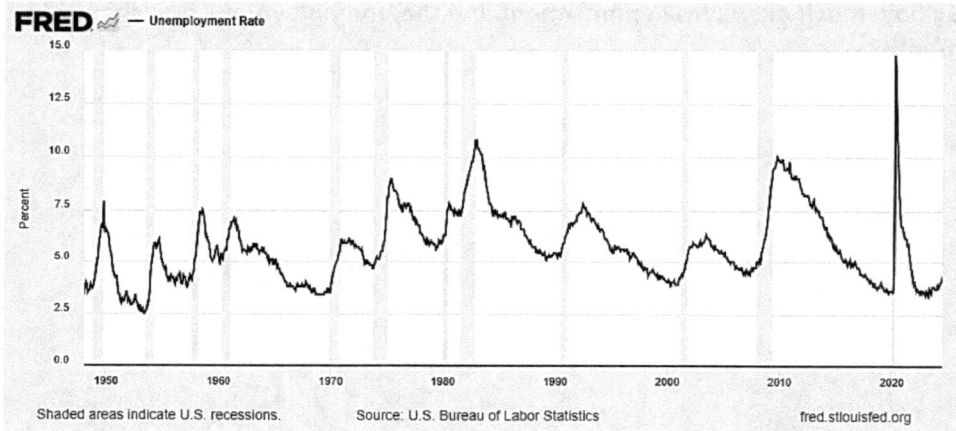

Chart 1-2. All Employees, Total Nonfarm (PAYEMS series, 1939-01-01 to 2024-
07-01). Monthly data.

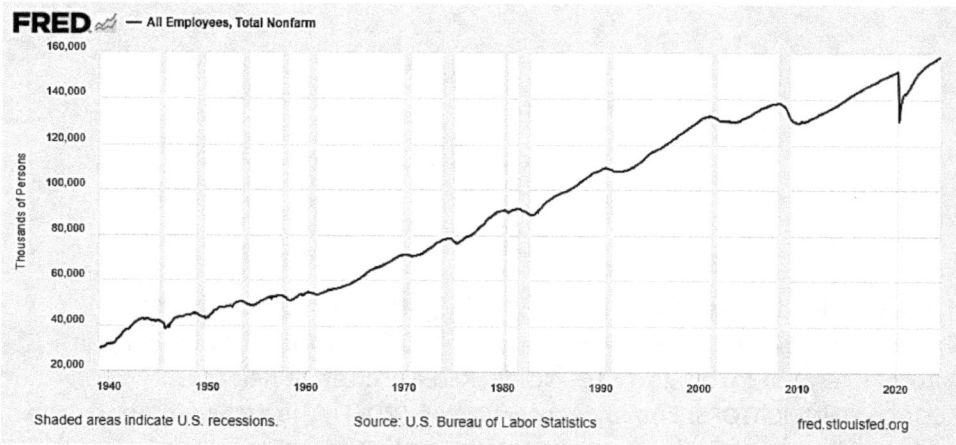

** Charts 1-1 (18) and 1-2 (19) replicate Charts 1-2 of the BLS jobs report (16)
and expand them to more years. They were generated by using FRED (17),
Federal Reserve Economic Data, Federal Reserve Bank of St. Louis, on 8/8/24.

2   GDP & Real GDP

2.1   Overview

The GPD (gross domestic product) measures the value of final goods and services produced in the United States.
The *real* GDP is its measure, after adjustment for the price level.

One of the things GDP omits is leisure. What does this mean?

Let's consider an example. Karen earns $50,000 in year 1 and $52,000 in year 2. The CPI in year 1 is 100 and the CPI in year 2 is 110. Since Karen's income rises by 4% and the price level by 10% between year 1 and year 2, we deduce that her income did *not* keep up with inflation.

How about leisure?

Let's assume she worked 50 hours a week for 52 weeks out of year 1: that's 2600 hours for year 1. Let's also assume she worked 40 hours a week for 50 weeks out of year 2: that's 2000 hours for year 2. This means she made $19.23/hour in year 1 and $26/hour in year 2. What do we conclude now? Karen's hourly wage rose by 35.2%, compared to an inflation rate of 10%: her hourly wage more than kept up with inflation!

In other words, in measuring how well off we are today, if we do not account for the fact that we have more leisure time today than we used to, we are underestimating our real income or real GDP!

The Bureau of Economic Analysis (BEA) produces the GDP numbers:
https://www.bea.gov/ (20)
The National Bureau of Economic Research (NBER) dates business cycles:
https://www.nber.org/ (21)
For the latest U.S. GDP numbers release, go to:
https://www.bea.gov/data/gdp/gross-domestic-product (22)

2.2   To-Do-List

- Sign in your online course.
- **Read your textbook chapter**. (required)
- **Complete your Graded Homework**. (required)

Recommended Mary J. McGlasson's Macroeconomics Module videos (optional) (7):

(Macro) Ep. 20: GDP (3:51) (23)
(Macro) Ep. 21: Real GDP (2:37) (24)

Recommended Marginal Revolution University (MRU) Principles of Macroeconomics videos (optional) (12):

GDP: What is Gross Domestic Product (GDP)? (4:35) (25)
GDP: Nominal vs. Real GDP (7:41) (26)

2.3   Econ. In the News: GDP versus GDI

In his 8/29/22 WSJ article (27), Jon Hilsenrath explains:

> Economic output can be measured two different ways: gross domestic
> product, or gross domestic income. For every dollar an individual spends
> to buy some good or service—a restaurant meal, a car, a doctor's visit—
> another individual earns a dollar of income to make and deliver that
> good or service. GDP captures the spending side of these transactions,
> GDI the income side.

Go to https://fred.stlouisfed.org/graph/?id=GDPC1,A261RX1Q020SBEA (28)
and https://fred.stlouisfed.org/series/A939RX0Q048SBEA (Charts 2-1 and 2-2)
(29)
Mouse over line charts 2-1 and 2-2 to read what the real GDP, real GDI & real
GDP per capita were last quarter.
Do YOU see much difference between real GDP and real GDI numbers?
Why would YOU be interested in GDP per capita as opposed to GDP? *

* GDP per capita accounts for population to better paint a picture of growth.
Still, can everyone be better off even if GDP per capita falls? Yes, argues Bryan
Caplan (3/27/05 EconLog post, (30)), taking the example of per-capita income.
Ten people can earn $50,000 per year, one year. The following year, these ten
earn $55,000 each, but another ten people entering the labor force, earn
$25,000 each—income per capita decreases even though everyone is better off.

Chart 2-1. Real GDP & real GDI (GDPC1 & A261RX1Q020SBEA series, 1947-01-01 to 2024-04-01). Quarterly data.

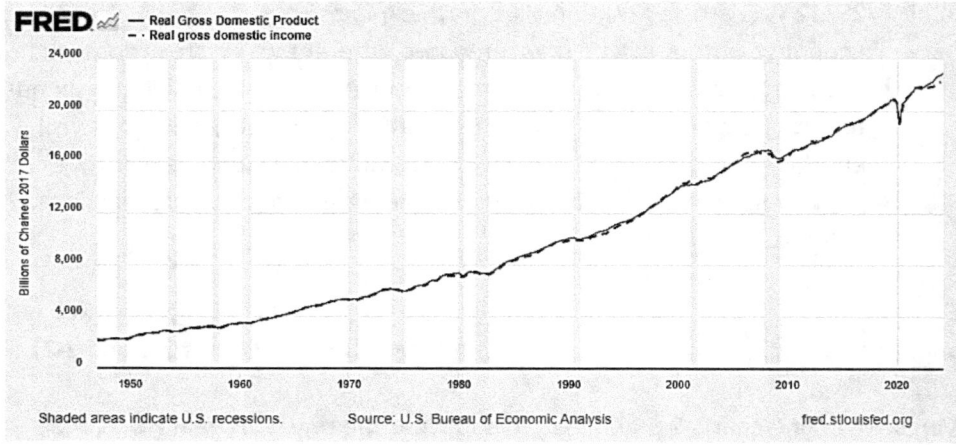

Chart 2-2. Real GDP per capita (A939RX0Q048SBEA series, 1947-01-01 to 2024-04-01). Quarterly data.

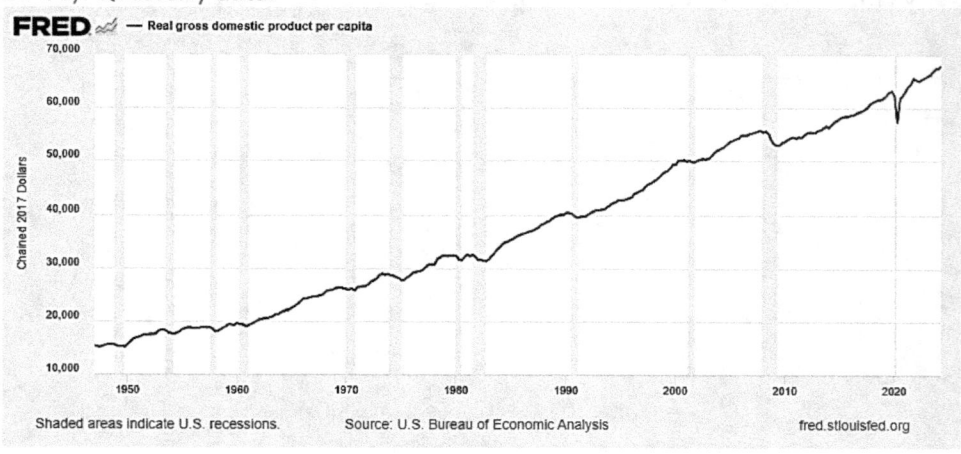

Charts 2-1 and 2-2 were generated on 8/8/24 using FRED (17), Federal Reserve Economic Data, Federal Reserve Bank of St. Louis.

3 Aggregate Demand & Aggregate Supply

3.1 Overview

Which comes first? The egg or the chicken? **The demand or the supply?**

Imagine you are stranded on a tropical island. Soon enough, you find yourself hungry and in a need of a shelter. How is your demand for food and shelter going to be met?

If you don't get your butt off your rock and start looking for some fruits to eat around the island, your consumption will stay at zero. Looks like you'll have to get yourself busy gathering branches to construct your shelter too, if you want to have one by nightfall. In other words, zero production means zero consumption. It looks like we've just been arguing that supply comes before demand, or production before consumption.

Does this make sense to YOU?

At a market level (microeconomics), a supply and demand framework is used to analyze the determinants of Demand (D) and Supply (S), and in turn, the equilibrium price and quantity prevailing in that market.

At the economy level (macroeconomics), a supply and demand framework is used to analyze the determinants of Aggregate Demand (AD) and Aggregate Supply (AS), and in turn, the price level and the real GDP level in that economy.

3.2 Econ. In the News: Consumption, Investment, Government Expenditures, Net Export.

Chart 1 is the plot of the four major components of GDP, or the determinants of AD, from 1947 to early 2024: consumption (C), investment (I), government purchases (G), and net export (NX)*.
https://fred.stlouisfed.org/graph/?id=PCECC96,GPDIC1,GCEC1,EXPGSC1,IMPGSC1** (Chart 3-1) (31)
The shape of the Consumption (C) line is consistent with the GDP/GDI line we've looked at in Section 2.3. **Does this make sense? Why or why not?** ***

Chart 3-1. C, I, G, NX (PCECC96, GPDIC1, GCEC1, EXPGSC1, IMPGSC1 series, 1947-01-01 to 2024-04-01). Quarterly data.

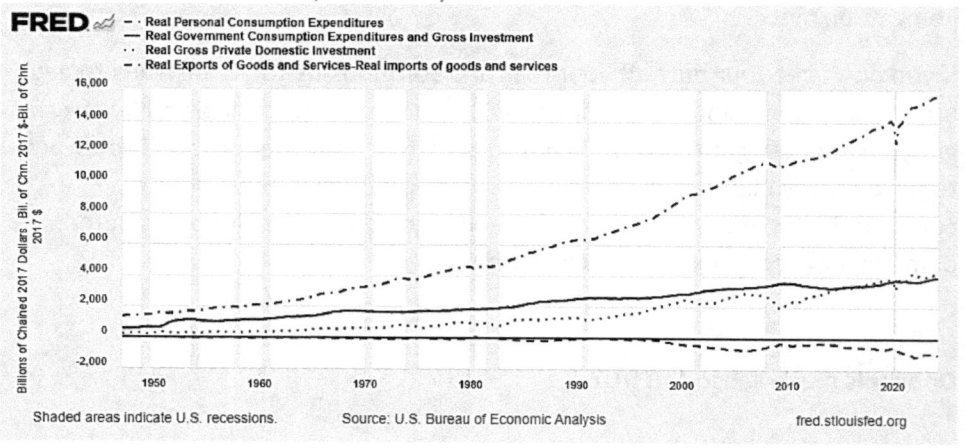

* For more information about the concepts and methods used to measure GDP and its components, please see the U.S. Bureau of Economic Analysis (BEA) NIPA Handbook (National Income and Product Accounts) (32) .
** This link (31) will take you to the graph of C (PCECC96 series), I (GPDIC1 series), G (GCEC1 series), EX (EXPGSC1 series) and IM (IMPGSC1 series). To get net export NX, go to EDIT GRAPH > EDIT LINE 4 > Add IMPGSC1 > Apply Formula a-b and next, Edit Line 5 > Delete. Chart 3-1 was generated on 8/8/24 using FRED (17), Federal Reserve Economic Data, Federal Reserve Bank of St. Louis.
*** This makes sense: C is the principal component of GDP. It is C that drives the shape of the GDP line.

4 Classical Macroeconomics

4.1 Overview

Although economies are unstable, classical economists trust the economy to self-adjust and to move back in the direction of full employment and optimal production level (GDP).

4.2 Econ. In the News: CPI Report

The U.S. Bureau of Labor Statistics (BLS) (1) releases a CPI report (33) to the public, monthly. It reports the *percentage change* of the CPI from the previous month, and from a year ago, as well as provides two charts we replicate, next. (We first spoke about the CPI (Consumer Price Index) in Section 1.1.)

Go to: https://www.bls.gov/news.release/pdf/cpi.pdf (33)*
Read the first paragraph about last month Consumer Price Index for All Urban Consumers (CPI-U).
By what percent did last month CPI change compared to the month before that and compared to a year before that?

* You can find the latest CPI report (33) by going to: bls.gov > SUBJECTS: Inflation & Prices: Consumer Price Index > CPI Publications: News Releases. Alternatively, go to: bls.gov > ECONOMIC RELEASES: Latest Releases > MAJOR ECONOMIC INDICATORS: Consumer Price Index (PDF). The archived reports can be found by going to: bls.gov > ECONOMIC RELEASES: Archived News Releases > Major Economic Indicators: Consumer Price Index (34).

Go to https://fred.stlouisfed.org/series/CPIAUCSL (used for Chart 4-1;
seasonally adjusted numbers) (35)**
Mouse over the line chart to read what the CPI was last month & *the month
before*. Compute the percentage change.
**Is the percentage change you get for last month CPI, consistent with what the
BLS reported?**

Chart 4-1. One-month percent change in CPI-U, seasonally adjusted (CPIAUCSL
series), Feb 1947-Jun 2024.

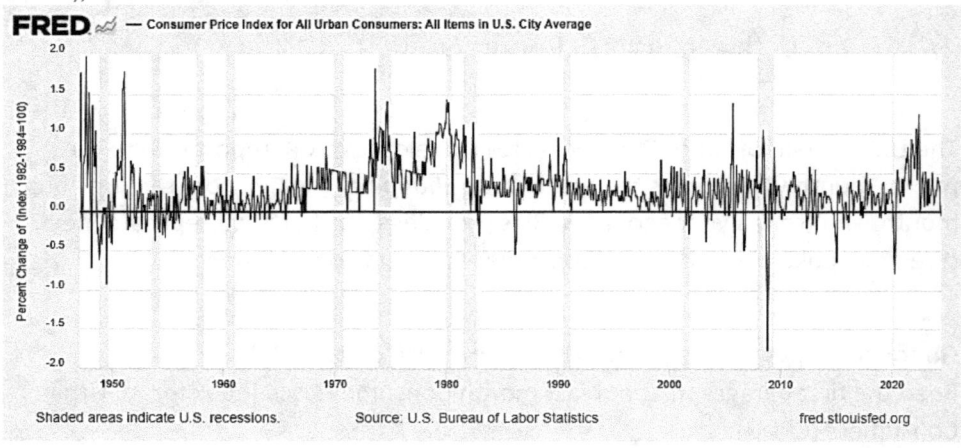

** This link (35) leads you to the graph of CPI-U, seasonally adjusted. Go to EDIT
GRAPH > EDIT LINE 1 and change Units to "Percent Change" to get the graph of
one-month change in CPI-U (Chart 4-1). Chart 4-1 was generated 8/8/24 using
FRED (17), Federal Reserve Economic Data, Federal Reserve Bank of St. Louis.

Go to https://fred.stlouisfed.org/series/CPIAUCNS (used for Charts 4-2 and 4-3; *not* seasonally adjusted numbers) (36)***

Mouse over the line chart to read what the CPI was last month & *12 months before*. Compute the percentage change.

Is the percentage change you get for last month CPI, consistent with what the BLS reported?

Mouse over the line chart to read what the CPI was Dec 2019 and Dec 2023. Compute the percentage change.

What is the percentage change in the price level in this four-year span? ****
How does that compare to past changes?

*** This link (36) leads you to the graph of CPI-U, not seasonally adjusted (Chart 4-3). Go to EDIT GRAPH > EDIT LINE 1 and change Units to "Percent Change from Year Ago" to get the graph of 12-month change in CPI-U (Chart 4-2).

**** ΔCPI = 306.746 − 256.974 = + 49.772; (+49.772/256.974)100 = + 19.37% (page consulted & calculation done 3/12/24).

Chart 4-2. 12-month percent change in CPI-U, not seasonally adjusted (CPIAUCNS series), Jan 1914-Jun 2024.

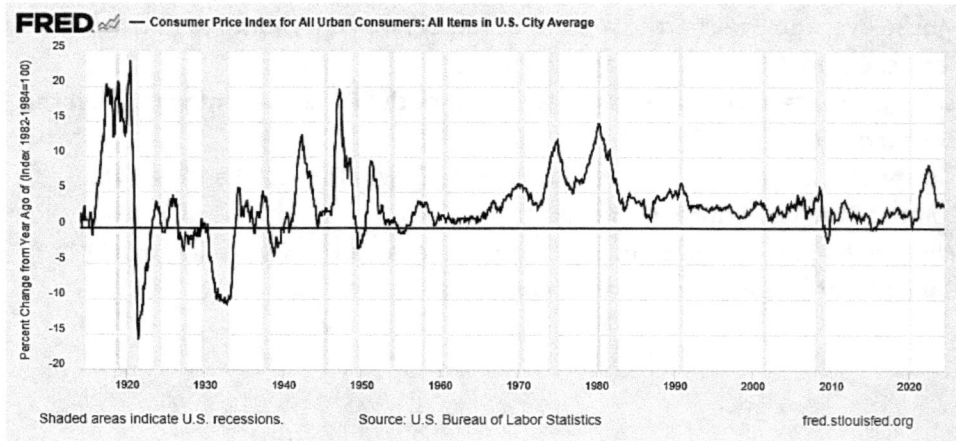

Shaded areas indicate U.S. recessions.   Source: U.S. Bureau of Labor Statistics   fred.stlouisfed.org

Chart 4-3. CPI for All Urban Consumers (CPI-U), not seasonally adjusted (CPIAUCNS series), Jan 1913-Jun 2024.

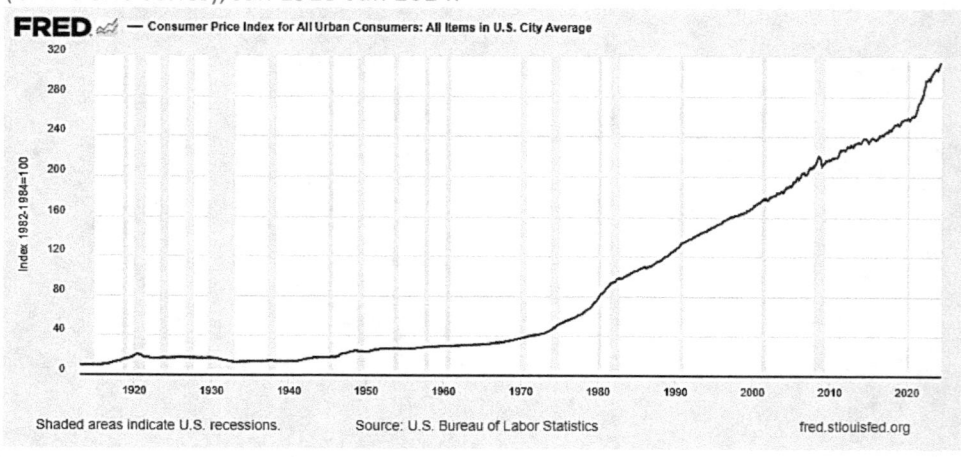

Shaded areas indicate U.S. recessions.   Source: U.S. Bureau of Labor Statistics   fred.stlouisfed.org

Charts 4-2 and 4-3 were generated 8/8/24 using FRED (17), Federal Reserve Economic Data, Federal Reserve Bank of St. Louis.

5   Keynesian Macroeconomics

5.1   Overview

Keynesians argue that government intervention is needed to move the economy back to full employment in a timely manner. Keynesians' main criticism of Classical Economists seem to hinge on the stickiness of prices (and most importantly, wages, which are the price of labor). Arnold et al. (37) state "Keynes said that the internal structure of an economy is not always competitive enough to allow prices to fall."

To fall???!!??

Prices rarely go down—rather, their increase slows down. Please, see Chart 3, in Section 4*.

What do YOU think prevents prices (including wages) from being flexible for the economy to self-adjust?

Can government intervention be timely? Can government intervention be the cause of price stickiness and economic instability?

Can YOU think of untimely or economically disruptive government interventions?

*WAIT! Chart 3, Section 4, is that of the CPI-U, which tracks the price level of the market basket that urban consumers buy—that's not the price of labor. How does the chart for <u>wages</u> look like?

One thing that the Classical Macroeconomics and Keynesian Macroeconomics models seem to have in common, as presented in most textbooks, is that neither of them explain how wealth is created.

How does the long-run GPD increase over time?

Recommended Marginal Revolution University (MRU) Principles of Macroeconomics video (12): The Keynesians (8:04) (38).

5.2 Econ. In the News: The Great Recession, The Great Lockdown, The Eras Tour & more.

5.2.1 The Great Recession (2007-09) & The Great Lockdown (2020)

Did you get a chance to think about examples of untimely or economically disruptive government interventions?

The 2007-09 great recession comes to mind. (Do you remember 2008? I do.) Rather than a failure of the free market, the subprime mortgage crisis, financial collapse and subsequent recession would have been created by government policies that pushed for greater homeownership (Daniel Press, 9/4/18 FEE article, (39)). A 40% increase in the minimum wage, implemented during that same period (U.S. Department of Labor, (40)), as well as policy such as increases or prolongation of unemployment benefits, prevented pressure down on wages, and subsequently, prices in general, which slowed down the recovery.

How about the 2020 great lockdown ("COVID-19 recession") …?? Economist Robert Mulligan, in a 7/20/21 AIER article (41), states the obvious—it was created by "profound" government restrictions. Mulligan also argues that "unprecedented recklessness for relief" were the seeds to the inflation that followed.

PLEASE, continue to be critical of the material presented to you: Does it make sense? Are the arguments sound/logical? Is the data relevant or complete? What are the underlying ethics? All individuals have unique knowledge that experts do not have: What is your personal experience? Look around you, what do you see? Does your assessment differ from that of experts? Why?

5.2.2 The Multiplier Effect: The Eras Tour (2023) vs Food Stamps

The Eras Tour is a concert tour by American singer-songwriter Taylor Swift. Like college students on spring break, fans go on a spending spree when Taylor Swift comes to town (7/23/23 Joseph Pisani's WSJ article (42)):

> Her fans have been filling hotels, packing restaurants and crowding bars during Swift's 20-city Eras Tour in the U.S. Cities say the tour has helped them recover from the economic toll of the pandemic by bringing back tourists and their wallets.

How does the (multiplier*) effect from Taylor Swift's fans spending spree differ from the (multiplier*) effect of governments spending spree on the economy? *Multiplier effect is the economic jargon for "snowball" effect.

In this 8/24/11 WSJ opinion piece (43), economist Robert J. Barro disagrees with the Agriculture Secretary Tom Vilsack's who believes the multiplier effect of food stamps is around two. Barro argues that food stamps are *not* economic stimulus, generating economic activity for every dollar of benefits spent. He explains that greater provision of social insurance and redistribution of income reduces GDP by incentivizing people (who receive and pay for the benefits) to work less, and by decreasing investment (due to diminished after tax return). How can the government improve things, compared to the market, by just borrowing money and giving it to people? Barro asks. He then offers empirical evidence: The steep increase in unemployment benefits in 2009 adversely affected the labor market.

6 Fiscal Policy & the Federal Budget

6.1 Overview

Classical economists trust the economy to self-adjust (see Section 4.1) while Keynesians tend to favor activist monetary and fiscal policy (see Section 5.1). Fiscal policy and the federal budget are the subject of this section*.

Go to https://www.bea.gov/itable/national-gdp-and-personal-income (44): Interactive Data Tables** > SECTION 3. Table 3.1. Government Current Receipts and Expenditures > Modify > Scale: Billions, Series: Annual, Select All Years, Refresh Table > Chart > Current Expenditures: Consumption expenditures, Current transfer payments, Interest payments, Subsidies. You should obtain a colorful line chart.

Mouse over the line chart and fill out the table below.

Billions of dollars	2019	2020	2021	2022	2023
Consumption expenditure					
Current transfer payments					
Interest payments					
Subsidies					

* Recommended Marginal Revolution University (MRU) Principles of Macroeconomics videos (12): Intro to Fiscal Policy (3:26) (45), The Best-Case Scenario (3:37) (46), Limits of Fiscal Policy (7:05) (47), Dangers of Fiscal Policy (6:02) (48), Crowding Out (5:25) (49).
** For a quick tour of BEA data tools, see Navigating BEA Interactive Data video (50).

By how much did transfer payments increase between 2019 and 2020? How much was that in percentage terms? ***

By how much did subsidies increase between 2019 and 2020? How much was that in percentage terms? ***

*** The BEA website was consulted on 3/12/24. Based on the numbers collected then, transfer payments increased by 1,107.4 billion dollars (1.1 trillion dollars) or 35%, and subsidies increased by 583.9 billion dollars or 800%.

Billions of dollars	2019	2020	2021	2022	2023
Consumption expenditure	3,014.9	3,178.3	3,366.3	3,570.1	3,752.2
Current transfer payments	3,162.9	4,270.3	4,648.4	4,020.5	4,112.8
Interest payments	883.5	815.3	855.5	973.7	1,239.1
Subsidies	73.0	656.9	482.7	127.4	101.1

6.2   Econ. In the News: Can Fiscal Policy Contribute to Inflation?

In MRU's The Dangers of Fiscal Policy video (51), Alex Tabarrok points out that fiscal policy could be effective when resources are underemployed due to an aggregate demand shock and the economy needs a short-run boost, but there is less agreement when it comes to using fiscal policy to combat supply shocks. The shutting down of the economy by our government in 2020 represented a real supply shock. This was accompanied by an unprecedented increase in transfer payments and subsidies (see Section 6.1). All this could create, Alex Tabarrok would argue, was much higher inflation.

Don Boudreaux, quoting Stanley Lebergott, states "inflation surfaced in 1968-69 when the federal government rapidly increased expenditure for both a war in Vietnam and a war on poverty at home. Over the next decade the voters revealed their desire for ever more programs of expenditure, and an almost equal desire to pay no increased taxes for such programs. Inflation proved a way to reconcile these conflicting desires" (6/19/22 Café Hayek post (52)).

John Cochrane states "any inflation target is (of course) a joint target of fiscal as well as monetary policy. Fiscal policy needs to commit to repay debt at the inflation target". In other words, "inflation control depends on fiscal policy too" (7/27/23 The Grumpy Economist post (53)).

In a 7/20/23 WSJ opinion piece (54), Mickey D. Levy argues that stimulating fiscal policies, "largest government spending programs directed at the nation's infrastructure and industry since the 1930s", require the Fed to raise rates further to achieve its inflation target.

In an 8/2/23 WSJ opinion piece (55), the Editorial Board argues that Fitch's downgrade (56) from AAA to AA+ was too kind.

> For evidence, consider how much the U.S. fiscal and political outlook has deteriorated since the previous debt downgrade in 2011. Standard & Poor's dropped its AAA rating on U.S. debt while Fitch and Moody's didn't. The ratio of U.S. debt held by the public to GDP at the time was only 65.5%, while the Congressional Budget Office expects it to be 98.2% this year. That's up from 79.4% before the pandemic. U.S. "general government debt" is more than two-and-a-half times greater than the median 39.6% of GDP for a AAA rating.

Did you know that Fitch Ratings, one of the major credit rating agencies, downgraded the US debt from AAA to AA+?

7 Money, Banking, & the Financial System

7.1 Overview

"*M1* describes the most liquid and widely accepted assets used to easily settle transactions: currency, demand deposits, and highly liquid accounts. **Before April 24, 2020, savings accounts were not part of M1. Limitations in the number of transfers from savings deposits made savings accounts less liquid than M1.**" (FRED Blog (57), Silva & Zimmermann's 5/20/21 post (58)). The limitation on the number of these transfers was lifted on April 24, 2020. Consequently, savings are now more liquid and part of "M1 money".

Below is the updated graph from that post:

Chart 7-1. Series M2SL, M1SL, CURRSL + DEMDEPSL + OCDSL (discontinued): Billions of Dollars (Jan 1959-Jun 2024).

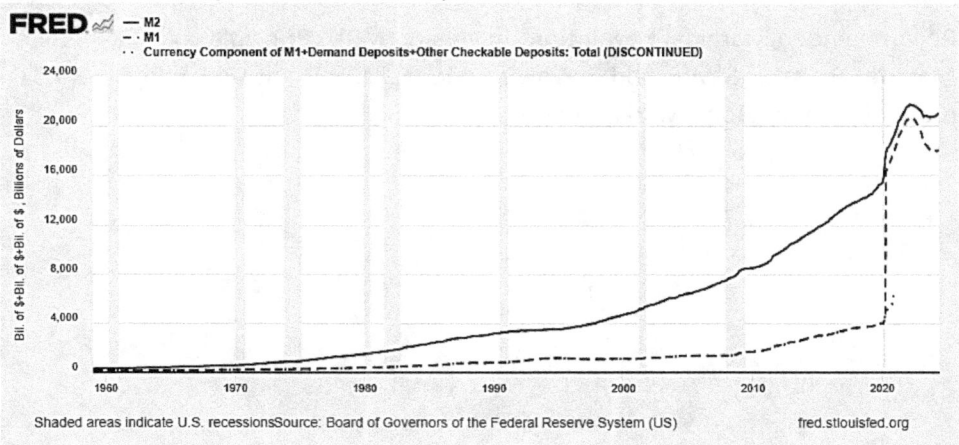

Chart 7-1 was generated on 8/8/24 via https://fred.stlouisfed.org/graph/?g=UIfc (59), using FRED (17), Federal Reserve Economic Data, Federal Reserve Bank of St. Louis. Note, the discontinued series is (dot line) follows the M1 series (dash line) up until the last few data points.

Using Arnold textbook terminology (37), the M1 and M2 definitions of money supply changed from:

M1 = currency held outside banks + demand deposits + other liquid deposits (*not* including savings deposits)

M2 = M1 + small-denomination time deposits + retail money market mutual funds

To:

M1 = currency held outside banks + demand deposits + other liquid deposits (**including savings deposits**)

M2 = M1 + small-denomination time deposits + retail money market mutual funds

Recommended Marginal Revolution University (MRU) Principles of Macroeconomics, Saving and Borrowing, videos (12): What Do Banks Do? (4:31) (60), Intro to the Bond Market (6:23) (61).

7.2   Econ. In the News: Money supply, Inflation & the Value of Money.

7.2.1   Money Supply

Go to https://fred.stlouisfed.org/series/M2SL (Charts 7-2 and 7-3) (62)
Mouse over the line chart to read what the level of money supply M2 was in
Mar & Apr 2020, and Feb & Mar 2023.
**What is the percentage change in M2 for April 2020 and March 2023,
compared to the month before? ***
Change the units of the chart to percent change**. Mouse over the line chart to
read Apr 2020 & Mar 2023 values.
How are those values compared to the ones you obtained above?

* M2 was 15,978.7 billion dollars in March 2020 and 16,997.7 in April 2020.
(16,997.7-15,978.7)/15,978.7 =1,019/15,978.7=0.0638 or 6.38%: M2 *increased*
at an unprecedented rate of 6.38% in April 2020. M2 was 15,978.7 billion dollars
in Feb 2023 and 16,997.7 in March 2023. (20,861,3-21,086.1.)/21,086.1 = -
224.8/21,086.1= - 0.01066 or - 1.07%: M2 *decreased* at an unprecedented rate
of 1.07% in March 2023.
** EDIT GRAPH > EDIT LINE 1 > Units: Percent Change.

Chart 7-2. Series M2SL: Billions of Dollars, Seasonally Adjusted, Monthly data (Jan 1959-Jun 2024).

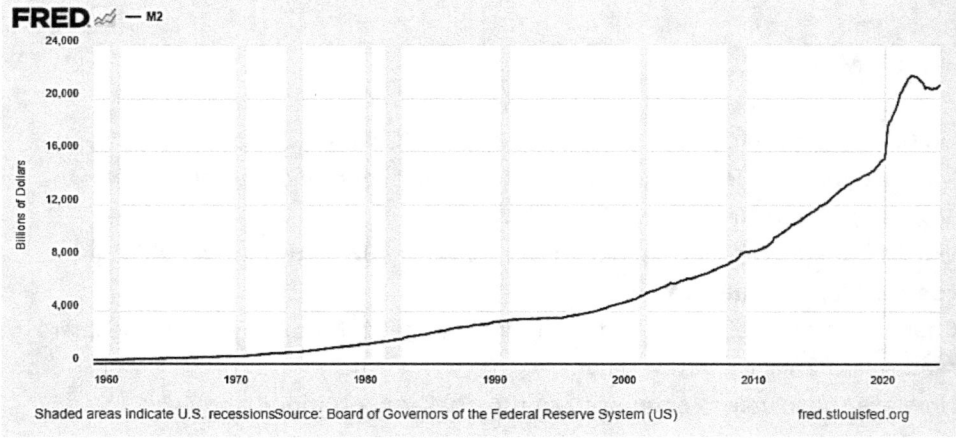

Chart 7-3. Series M2SL: Percent Change of Billions of Dollars, Seasonally Adjusted, Monthly data (Feb 1959-Jun 2024).

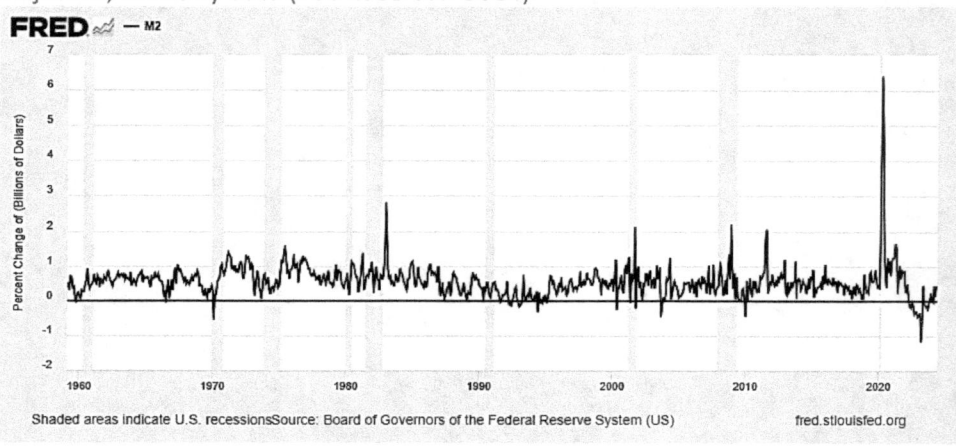

Charts 7-2 and 7-3 were generated on 8/8/24 using FRED (17), Federal Reserve Economic Data, Federal Reserve Bank of St. Louis.

7.2.2   Inflation & the Value of Money

On a 3/17/24 post on Substack (63), John Cochrane points to a Feb 2024 National Bureau of Economic Research (NBER) (64) working paper by Bolhuis et al. (65). It outlines the fact that the way the cost of housing is computed, when measuring inflation, changed in 1983. The main difference, Cochrane explains, is that the old measure counts the price and interest rate you have to pay to buy a new house as the cost of the house, while the new measure is based on what it costs to rent a house. Figure 7, from Bolhuis et al.'s working paper is copied below (Chart 7-4).

What do you think the rationale behind the U.S. Bureau of Labor Statistics (BLS) change in methodology was?

How do you think the change in the way the cost is computed affects the estimates of housing inflation today?

What is the right way to compute inflation?

Chart 7-4. Figure 7 from Bolhuis et al.'s working paper.

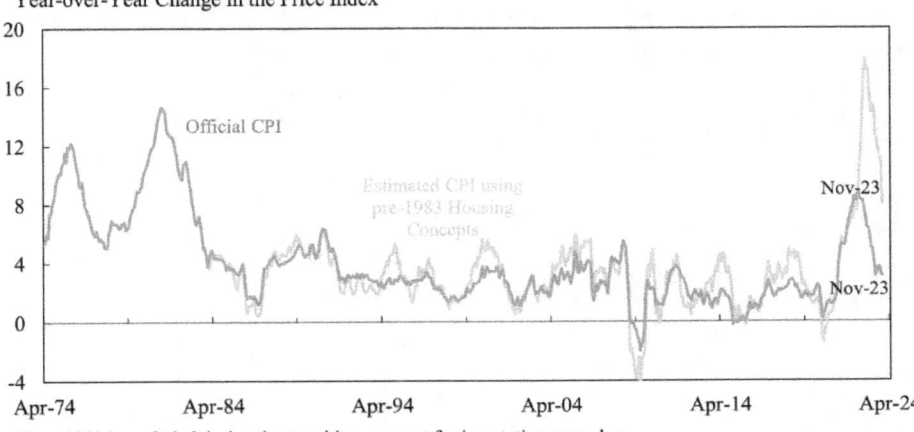

Official and Estimated CPI using pre-1983 housing methods, 1974-2023
Year-over-Year Change in the Price Index

Note: 1983 is excluded during the transition, see text for imputation procedure.
Source: Bureau of Labor Statistics; Authors' Calculations.

8   The Federal Reserve System

8.1   Overview

The Federal Reserve System (66) is the central bank of the United States. It performs five general functions to promote the effective operation of the U.S. economy and, more generally, the public interest. The Federal Reserve

- conducts the nation's monetary policy to promote maximum employment, stable prices, and moderate long-term interest rates in the U.S. economy;
- promotes the stability of the financial system and seeks to minimize and contain systemic risks through active monitoring and engagement in the U.S. and abroad;
- promotes the safety and soundness of individual financial institutions and monitors their impact on the financial system as a whole;
- fosters payment and settlement system safety and efficiency through services to the banking industry and the U.S. government that facilitate U.S.-dollar transactions and payments; and
- promotes consumer protection and community development through consumer-focused supervision and examination, research and analysis of emerging consumer issues and trends, community economic development activities, and the administration of consumer laws and regulations.

8.2   Econ. In the News: Adding Racial Equity and Climate Change to The Fed's Mandates?

The three economic goals the Federal Reserve (67) pursue are "maximum employment, stable prices, and moderate long-term interest rates".

House Bill H.R. 2543 (68) would add racial equity to the Fed's mandates. It passed the House 215-207 on 6/15/22* (WSJ article, 6/21/22 (69)). The **bill** would require "the Federal Reserve Board to carry out its duties in a manner that supports the elimination of racial and ethnic disparities in employment, income, wealth, and access to affordable credit. The board must report on disparities in labor force trends as well as on plans and activities of the board to minimize and eliminate these disparities." The WSJ Editorial Board warns, "Central bankers have a hard enough time balancing full employment with stable prices. Adding a racial equity mandate could cause their models to go catawampus. How small would the black-white unemployment gap have to be, and how high would prices have to climb, before the Fed considers raising interest rates?"

Were you aware that the U.S. is considering such changes to its central bank's mandates?

* Senate Bill S.1327 (70) – Federal Reserve Racial and Economic Equity Act was first introduced in the Senate 4/22/21. Senate Bill S.2257 (71) – Federal Reserve Racial and Economic Equity Act introduced in the Senate again on 7/12/23.

In a 12/02/22 press release (72), the Federal Reserve Board invited public comment on proposed principles regarding exposures to climate-related financial risks for large banking organizations. The Federal Register's notice published on 12/08/22 (73) states that the principles are intended to support efforts by large financial institutions to focus on key aspects of climate-related financial risk management. In a statement released 12/02/22 (74), Governor Waller indicates he does not support the issuance of guidance on climate change. He explains, "I disagree with the premise that climate change poses a serious risk to the safety and soundness of large banks and the financial stability of the United States. The Federal Reserve conducts regular stress tests on large banks that impose extremely severe macroeconomic shocks and they show that the banks are resilient."

On 1/10/23, following US Fed Chair Jerome H. Powell's Stockholm speech (Panel 3. 30:42-35:35) (75)** at the International Symposium organized by Sveriges Riksbank, Sweden's central bank (76), John Cochrane (aka The Grumpy Economist) gives cheers for Powell. He points out the following excerpts from his speech***:

> ...Decisions about policies to directly address climate change should be made by the elected branches of government and thus reflect the public's will as expressed through elections.

> ... without explicit congressional legislation, it would be inappropriate for us to use our monetary policy or supervisory tools to promote a greener economy or to achieve other climate-based goals. We are not, and will not be, a "climate policymaker."

** The written speech by Chair Powell on central bank independence is available on The Federal Reserve website, (77).
*** For more on John Cochrane's comments about Powell's Stockholm speech, see his 1/10/23 blog post, Cheers for Powell (78).

9 Money & the Economy

9.1 Overview

The equation of exchange is an identity stating that the money supply (M) times velocity (V) must equal the price level (P) times real GDP. In other words, the price tag of our domestically produced goods and services depends on how much money we have circulating in our economy. So, if our money supply growth follows our real GDP growth, we are good.

Chart 9-1. Series GDP&C1: Billions of (Chained 2017) Dollars, Seasonally Adj. Annual Rate, Quarterly (Q1 2010-Q2 2024).

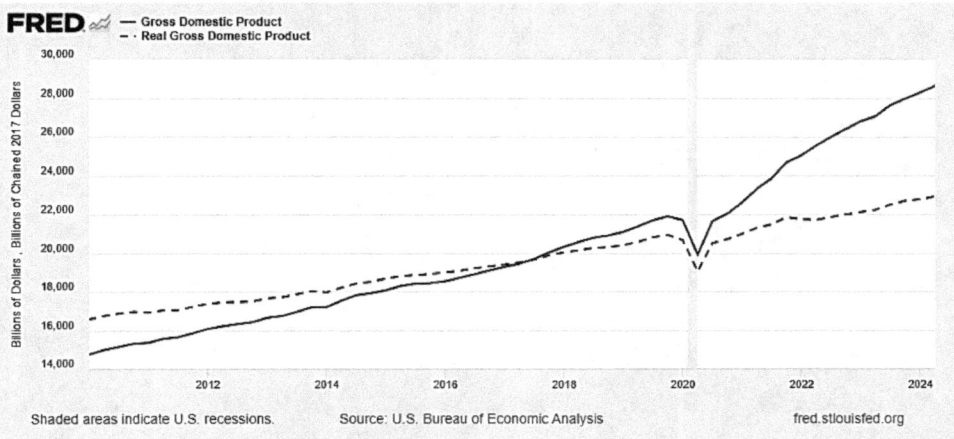

Chart 9-1 was generated via https://fred.stlouisfed.org/graph/?id=GDP,GDPC1 (79), on 8/8/24, using FRED (17), Federal Reserve Economic Data, Federal Reserve Bank of St. Louis. The starting date for that graph was changed from 1947-01-01 to Jan 2010.

What happens if we shut our economy down and, at the same time, through at it more money?

If our money supply grows faster than our real GDP, then, our price level increases faster (inflation)—i.e., the difference between our (nominal) GDP and real GDP increases. Does Chart 9-1 show that this might have happened?

What else could have triggered an increasing difference between our nominal and real GDP?

How about if we restrict our money supply? Can it slow down growth?

What else in our equation of exchange could have changed over that Q1 2020-Q2 2024 period? What's left? *

Did shutting down the economy decrease or increase velocity? Did lifting the limitations in the number of transfers from savings deposits decrease or increase velocity? Would a higher interest rate, which incentivize savings and disincentivize investments, decrease or increase velocity?

* Recommended Marginal Revolution University (MRU) Principles of Macroeconomics video (12): Quantity Theory of Money (3:27) (80).

9.2 Econ. In the News: Monetarism & Zimbabwe

Do you remember we pointed out that the money supply (M2) increased at an unprecedented rate in April 2020 and decreased at an unprecedented rate in March 2023? (See Section 7.3)

In this 6/22/22 WSJ article (81), Greg Ip argues that Nobel Prize-winning economist, Milton Friedman, who famously declared that inflation is always and everywhere a monetary phenomenon, is having a moment: "Surging money supply and inflation have Mr. Friedman's followers declaring, I told you so."

In this 10/21/22 WSJ article (82), Jon Hilsenrath explains that "recency bias" might have been at work when policy makers made the mistake of "flooded the economy and the financial system with money during and after the Covid crisis, leading to inflation". He points out, "Ms. Yellen now concedes that she misread the situation."

How does this make you feel?

In this 10/6/23 WSJ article (83), James Mackintosh points out that while some on Wall Street predict bad times because of an unprecedented drop in the money supply, Isabel Schnabel, a member of the European Central Bank (ECB) executive board, disagrees. She argues that the drop in M2 reflects a rebalancing of savings into higher-interest accounts and assets, and consequently, is not concerning.

Did you get a chance to view the video about Zimbabwe & Hyperinflation (see Section 1.2)? (4:19) (14)

In a 4/5/24 WSJ article (84), Gabriele Steinhauser reports that The Reserve Bank of Zimbabwe is launching a new national currency. The Zimbabwe dollar, launched in 2019, most recently traded at more than 30,674 units for one U.S. dollar. The new unit, the Zimbabwe Gold (ZiG), will be initially valued at 13.56 ZiGs for $1, and later at a rate determined by the market. The new currency is to be "fully backed by Zimbabwe's reserves of U.S. dollars and precious metals, particularly gold". John Mushayavanhu, Zimbabwe central bank's new governor, also pledged to end a long-running practice of the bank issuing more money to finance government spending: "We want a solid and stable national currency. It does not help to print money. Certainly, under my watch it is not going to happen." Gift Mugano, director at the Centre for African Governance Development, said that, for Zimbabwe to have a stable currency, the government first needs to bring its spending in line with what it raises through taxes and other income."

10 Monetary Policy

10.1 Overview

Economists disagree under what conditions, *if any*, monetary policy can bring about price stability, low unemployment, and economic growth.

Keynesians think money supply first affects interest rates, via the money market, and then leads to changes in investment and thus, AD, and, finally, price, employment and GDP levels. "Activists" (mostly Keynesians) favor using discretionary monetary policy to fine-tune the economy.

Monetarists think money supply directly leads to changes in AD, via increased consumption, and next, price, employment and GDP levels. "Nonactivist" (mostly monetarists) favor rules-based monetary policy, such as The Taylor Rule or average inflation targeting.

Recommended Marginal Revolution University (MRU) Principles of Macroeconomics video (12): Monetary Policy and the Fed (3:01) (85).

10.2 Econ. In the News: Gold Standard vs Fiat Money, FOMC Statement, Monetary Policy & U.S. Debt

In a WSJ 8/2/21 Opinion piece (86), professors Luther and Salter argue the Fed-managed fiat dollar hasn't lived up to its potential. They believe the Fed could mimic how the money supply adjusted automatically on the gold standard* by adopting a strict monetary rule to accommodate changes in money demand.

The Federal Open Market Committee (FOMC (87)) statement, issued 11/2/22 (88), indicates that "the Committee decided to raise the target range for the federal funds rate to 3-3/4 to 4 percent". In his press conference writing statement, on 11/2/22 (89)**, Chair Powell explains that the goal is to bring inflation down. He reiterates, "We will stay the course, until the job is done."

In this June 13, 2023 WSJ article (90), July Shelton notes how much rising interest rates have increased the cost of servicing U.S. government debt:

> In July 2021, the Congressional Budget Office (CBO) projected (91) the 10-year cost of servicing U.S. government debt for 2022-31 at $5.43 trillion. In May 2023, the CBO estimated that the cost for 2024-33 will be $10.56 trillion (92).

* Under a gold standard, a monetary unit is defined as a specific quantity of gold. Coins, notes and deposit balances, used in transactions, have redeemable claims to gold. The 1944 Bretton Woods system limited redemption of dollars for gold to foreign governments. The redeemability of dollars for gold ended Aug 15, 1971 when fiat money was adopted.
** FOMC Press Conferences recordings can be found on the Federal Reserve YouTube channel (93): FOMC Press Conferences playlist (94).

11 Expectations Theory & the Economy

11.1 Overview

The following questions are addressed:

- Is there a stable relationship between inflation and unemployment? (The Phillips curve)
- What role do individuals' expectations, if any, play in that relationship?

Other important questions that need to be addressed include:

- What role do government policies, if any, play in that relationship?
- What factor others than individuals' expectations and government policies influence that relationship?
- How relevant are inflation and unemployment to individuals?
- Are different individuals, affected differently by inflation and unemployment?
- Which is best and to whom: High inflation and low unemployment, or low inflation and high unemployment?
- Does the answer to the last question depend on how a given level of inflation and unemployment come about?

What other questions do YOU think need to be addressed?

11.2 Econ. In the News: Expectations Theory & Policies, FRB/US, the U of Michigan Surveys of Consumers

In their 6/29/22 WSJ article (95), Nick Timiraos and Tom Fairless report on Federal Reserve Chairman Jerome Powell about the Fed monetary policy. They explained: "Fed officials are raising rates at the most aggressive pace since the 1980s in part because of concerns that higher prices could change consumer psychology in ways that sustain high inflation. Economists believe expectations of future inflation can be self-fulfilling." What is at the root of the approach adopted by the Fed is "the fear that households and businesses will come to expect high inflation to persist, which causes it to do so" explains Timiraos in his 7/5/22 article (96).

John Cochrane, via his 10/25/22 post on The Grumpy Economist blog (97), asks: Is inflation inherently unpredictable? Are we collectively in thrall of the same wrong model?

In a 4/18/24 WSJ article (98), Joseph C. Sternberg argues that the Fed's failure to predict accelerating inflation in 2021 is the central bank's model of the economy, FRBUS (99), which overemphasizes the role of everyone's expectations of future inflation as an input into current inflation.

The University of Michigan Survey Research Center (100) conducts monthly Surveys of Consumers (101). According to its April 2024 final results*, year-ahead inflation expectations ticked up from 2.9% last month to 3.2% this month. Long-run inflation expectations also edged up, from 2.8% last month to 3.0% this month; they have been within the narrow 2.9-3.1% range for 29 of the last 33 months. Long-run inflation expectations remain elevated relative to the 2.2-2.6% range seen in the two years pre-pandemic.

* This webpage was consulted on 4/30/24. Those most recent Survey of Consumers Attitudes (SCA) results can also be found via the Economic Behavior section of the Center, (102). Archived reports can be found via the data section of the Surveys of Consumers Attitudes site, (103).

12 Economic Growth, Creative Destruction & Crony Capitalism

12.1 Overview

It seems we've come full circle.

Do you remember Section 3?

We asked: Which comes first? The egg or the chicken? The demand or the supply?

We reasoned: Imagine you are stranded on a tropical island. Soon enough, you find yourself hungry and in a need of a shelter. How is your demand for food and shelter going to be met? If you don't get your butt off your rock and start looking for some fruits to eat around the island, your consumption will stay at zero. Looks like you'll have to get yourself busy gathering branches to construct your shelter too, if you want to have one by nightfall.

We concluded: Zero production means zero consumption. Production comes before consumption. Supply before demand.

Economic growth comes about by the increasingly efficient use of our resources and, while the price tag of that GDP is irrelevant, policies that de-incentivize putting resources to good use or re-direct resources use, are not.

Creative destruction is key to economic growth. It brings heartaches (job loss) but also opportunities (job creation). The fact that this process is ever-changing leads to fortunes changing hands quickly* and offers EVERY individual the opportunity to thrive, no matter their background!

*This also explains rent seeking behaviors—from those who do not want fortunes to change hands nor want to update their skills to keep up with changes.

12.2 Econ. In the News: Supply-Side Reforms, Creative Destruction vs Renewal, Corporate Welfare

12.2.1 Econ. In the News: Growth, Are Supply-Side Reforms Needed?

On 10/25/22 (104), on his Grumpy Economist's blog, John Cochrane talks about Liz Truss' pro-growth agenda as British prime minister (Sept-Oct 2022). He thinks the UK desperately needs supply-side reforms and Truss's proposed reforms were too mild.

> A 40% top marginal income tax rate (down from 45%) would not make the UK a low-tax free-market Shangri-La, especially considering that it would also still have a 20% value-added tax (VAT), national insurance taxes, property taxes, corporate taxes, and more. Recall that US President Ronald Reagan and Speaker of the House Tip O'Neill (a Democrat) cut the top federal marginal rate from 70% to 28%.

> Truss also proposed free-market "investment zones". But if one accepts that pro-investment tax and planning conditions are good in blighted areas, why not the whole country?

In announcing her policies, continues Cochrane, neither her nor her chancellor, Kwarteng, explained that "lower tax rates improve the incentives to work, save, invest, start a business, or, in the case of corporate taxes, move a business to the UK or keep it there. (Ideally, one cuts tax rates but broadens the base, maintaining revenues until spending falls.)"

Because over-regulation and restrictions are hobbling supply, Truss and Kwarteng pro-growth agenda included regulatory reforms in housing, labor, and energy production. Currently, argues Cochrane, Britain's housing restrictions, as in the US, lead to absurdly high prices, which stymies many businesses and the workers they might hire and is especially harmful to less-advantaged people who cannot afford to live near high-productivity jobs. Labor regulations are straitjacketing workplaces and social-program disincentives lead some people not to work at all.

In response to a global energy crisis, explains Cochrane, Truss had planned to bring back North Sea oil production and lift the UK's ban on fracking.

In a 4/18/24 WSJ Opinion Piece (105), economist R. Glenn Hubbard (Columbia Business School) points out that growth "requires an openness to change that is rare in a political climate stuck in past grievances". "Policymakers' hyperattention to those buffeted by change invites rent-seeking behavior and costly regulatory micromanagement."

Do you know of somewhat opposites arguments about growth, taxes and regulations?

Which one(s) do you find more compelling? (Logical?)

12.2.2 Econ. In the News: Growth, Creative Destruction or Creative Renewal?

In their Mostly Weekly Series Finale video (7:57) (106), Andrew Heaton and Sarah Rose Siskind talk about how new technology has created economic growth, increased our standard of living, creating new jobs and displacing old ones.

Enjoy!

12.2.3 Econ. In the News: Corporate Welfare

On a 7/19/22 Cafe Hayek's post (107), Don Boudreaux points to a 7/19/22 WSJ article (108) where "the Editorial Board decries the now-fashionable practice of using China's self-destructive economic policies as an excuse for U.S. corporate welfare". Boudreaux highlights the following three slices from the WSJ article:

> Industrial policy is back in fashion in Washington, or as it ought to be called, corporate welfare. The semiconductor industry is first in the queue, but it won't be the last. Taxpayers should at least know they'll be subsidizing highly profitable companies that don't need the help and might end up regretting the political handcuffs they're acquiring.

> The bill that will head to the Senate floor as early as Tuesday includes $52.2 billion in grants to the computer chip industry. But wait, there's more. Congress is also offering a 25% tax credit for semiconductor fabrication, which is estimated to cost about $24 billion over five years. That's $76 billion for one industry*.

> The other claim for the bill is that the U.S. must subsidize domestic chip-making to compete with China, but this also isn't persuasive. The companies like to point out that the U.S. share of the world's chips has fallen to 12% from 37% in 1990. They don't mention that the U.S. leads in chip design (52%) and chip-making equipment (50%). Seven of the world's 10 largest semiconductor companies are based in the U.S. China trails American companies by years in semiconductor technology.

* The CHIPS and Science Act (where CHIPS stands for "Creating Helpful Incentives to Produce Semiconductors") was signed into law on August 9, 2022; H.R.4346 (109).

History shows that easy government money can undermine competitiveness. It often leads to inefficient spending and investment. The politicians will also attach their own strings, perhaps with limits on stock buybacks and dividends.

The chip bill isn't needed to compete with China, and it will set a precedent that other industries will follow. Anybody who can throw up a China competition angle will ask for money.

In this 4/3/24 WSJ opinion piece (110), the Editorial Board reports that the U.S. chip maker Intel now says it will need even more subsidies, as it loses money on its foundry business. They point out that Intel CEO Pat Gelsinger was among the loudest advocates for Washington's $280 billion chips bill in 2022 to boost domestic chip manufacturing.

13 International Finance

13.1 Overview

The **foreign exchange market** is the market in which currencies of different countries are exchanged. In this market **currencies are bought and sold** for a price—this is **the exchange rate, the price of a currency relative to another**.

13.1.1 Overview: Where do the supply and demand for currencies come from?

Let's take the example of the market for American dollars in terms of Mexican pesos. In this market the demand* comes from Mexicans who need American dollars to buy American goods and the supply** comes from Americans who need Mexican pesos to buy Mexican goods. * *And people from other nations who hold Mexican pesos and want to exchange them for American dollars.* ** *And people from other nations who hold American dollars and want to exchange them for Mexican pesos.*

13.1.2 Overview: How is the exchange rate or price of a currency relative to another determined?

Under a flexible exchange rate system, like in any other market, the price is determined by the supply and demand.

13.1.3 Overview: What does it mean for a currency to appreciate or depreciate?

A currency appreciates when its price relative to another increases. In our example, if the demand for American dollars increases relatively more than the supply of American dollars, then this market equilibrium price increases—the price of the dollar in terms of pesos is higher: it takes more pesos to buy a dollar than it used to. The American dollar has appreciated. In other words, the dollar is worth more pesos than it used to.

A currency depreciates when its price relative to another decreases. In our example, if the supply of American dollars increases relatively more than the demand for American dollars, then this market equilibrium price decreases—the price of the dollar in terms of pesos is lower: it takes less pesos to buy a dollar than it used to. The American dollar has depreciated. In other words, the dollar is worth less pesos than it used to.

13.1.4 Overview: If currency A appreciates relative to currency B, what happens to currency B?

If the American dollar appreciates relative to the Mexican pesos, its price in terms of pesos is higher: it takes more pesos to buy a dollar than it used to. Inversely, it would take less dollars to buy one peso—the price of a peso in terms of dollars is lower. If the American dollar depreciates relative to the Mexican pesos, its price in terms of pesos is lower: it takes less pesos to buy a dollar than it used to. Inversely, it would take more dollars to buy one peso—the price of a peso in terms of dollars is higher.

If currency A appreciates relative to currency B, then currency B depreciates relative to currency A (& vice versa).

13.1.5 Overview: If A experiences inflation, what happens to the exchange rate of A relative to B?

If the U.S. price level increases relatively more than the Mexico price level does: it takes more dollars to buy goods & services than it used to. The American dollar has depreciated in terms of what it can buy***—including pesos, which is going to be reflected in the exchange rate: It will take more dollars to buy one peso****. *** Decrease in purchasing power. **** The PPP or purchasing power parity theory states that exchange rates between any two currencies adjust to reflect changes in the relative price levels of the two countries.*

Sounds just like any other market, doesn't it? What do YOU think?

13.1.6 Overview: What's the difference between a flexible and a fixed exchange rate system?

Under a flexible system, exchange rates would be solely determined by the supply and demand for a currency. Under a fixed exchange rate system, a nation's currency would be set at a fixed rate relative to all other currencies, and central banks would intervene in the foreign exchange market to maintain the fixed rate. **Today's international monetary system is described as a managed flexible exchange rate system or managed float**. The current system operates under flexible exchange rates, but not completely: governments justify interventions in the name of bringing stability to the exchange rates.

13.2 Econ. In the News: International Finance.

13.2.1 Econ. In the News: Flexible, fixed or managed flexible international monetary system?

In this 11/22/22 WSJ article (111), Paul Hannon notes that the Organization for Economic Cooperation and Development (OECD) (112) is advising the European Central Bank (ECB) (113) to raise its key interest rate to bring down inflation.

Because of higher energy prices, inflation in the eurozone has overtaken that in the U.S. and the bloc's common currency has lost ground against the dollar, explains Hannon. He further reports that Mr. Pereira, OECD's acting chief economist, said Europe would need higher interest rates to support the euro's exchange rate against the dollar and prevent a larger rise in prices of imported goods and services due to the currency's weakness.

13.2.2 Econ. In the News: How does the U.S. trade deficit relate to the strength of the dollar?

Transactions across countries include exchange of goods and services, but also exchange of factor services (labor, land, *and capital*). This means a strong dollar leads to trade deficits, both of which are a sign of a strong economy. Economist Don Boudreaux explains below (4/16/23 blog post, (114)).

> U.S. trade deficits arise because foreigners invest in the U.S. some of the dollars they earn on their export sales to Americans rather than spend all of these dollars immediately on purchases of American exports. Because the size of neither the world's nor any country's capital stock is fixed, such foreign investment can expand America's capital stock (in part by offsetting its diminution by our fiscally irresponsible government). If this expansion of our capital stock is in fact occurring, we Americans are made wealthier, not poorer. Increased savings and investment in America by non-Americans makes us wealthier no less than does increased savings and investment in America by Americans.

On a 4/25/23 blog post (115), Boudreaux quotes Dan Griswold and Andreas Freytage:

> The balance of trade points to the nation's strength as a haven for global investment, to robust trade in goods and services, and to a strong dollar that remains at the center of the global economy.

> The U.S. balance of trade in goods and, more broadly, the current account, have been in deficit for decades. Year after year, Americans buy more goods in global markets than they sell. The United States can only run a persistent deficit in its current account because it runs an equally persistent surplus in the financial account, which measures the flow of capital across the border. More investment flows into the United States each year than flows out, on net, in large part because the United States remains a safe and profitable haven for the world's savings. The investment, in turn, fuels growth and job creation.

References

1. **U.S. Bureau of Labor Statistics (BLS).** [Online] https://www.bls.gov/.

2. —. Consumer Price Index (CPI) Databases. [Online] https://www.bls.gov/cpi/data.htm.

3. —. Current Population Survey (CPS). [Online] https://www.bls.gov/cps/.

4. —. Report 1092: Women in the Labor Force: A Databook. [Online] April 2021. https://www.bls.gov/opub/reports/womens-databook/2020/pdf/home.pdf.

5. —. Consumer Price Index (CPI) Archived Supplemental Files. [Online] https://www.bls.gov/cpi/tables/supplemental-files/.

6. —. Annual Report: Women in the Labor Force: A Databook. [Online] https://www.bls.gov/cps/demographics.htm#women.

7. **McGlasson, Mary J.** Macroeconomics modudes playlist. *mjmfoodie YouTube channel.* [Online] https://www.youtube.com/playlist?list=PLF2A3693D8481F442.

8. —. (Macro) Episode 16: Inflation & Price Indexes (9:20). *mjmfoodie YouTube channel.* [Online] https://www.youtube.com/watch?v=SmOMp8gycMA&list=PLF2A3693D8481F442&index=16&t=2s.

9. —. (Macro) Episode 17: Real Income (5:24). *mjmfoodie YouTube channel.* [Online] https://www.youtube.com/watch?v=cwBpq5TOks0&list=PLF2A3693D8481F442&index=17.

10. —. (Macro) Episode 18: Unemployment (2:51). *mjmfoodie YouTube channel.* [Online] https://www.youtube.com/watch?v=_CdTu1pk06w&list=PLF2A3693D8481F442&index=18&t=1s.

11. —. (Macro) Episode 19: Types of Unemployment (4:20). *mjmfoodie YouTube channel.* [Online] https://www.youtube.com/watch?v=ZckAN1KYB5I&list=PLF2A3693D8481F442&index=19&t=1s.

REFERENCES

12. **Marginal Revolution University (MRU).** Principles of Economics: Macroeconomics. [Online] https://mru.org/principles-economics-macroeconomics-0.

13. —. Unemployment & Labor Force Participation: Is Unemployment Undercounted? (5:18) Instructor: Alex Tabarrok. [Online] https://mru.org/courses/principles-economics-macroeconomics/us-unemployment-rate-undercounted.

14. —. Inflation & Quantity Theory of Money: Zimbabwe and Hyperinflation (4:19). Instructor: Alex Tabarrok. [Online] https://mru.org/courses/principles-economics-macroeconomics/zimbabwe-currency-inflation.

15. —. Inflation & Quantity Theory of Money: Price Confusion & Money Illusion (5:04). Instructor: Alex Tabarrok. [Online] https://mru.org/courses/principles-economics-macroeconomics/costs-of-inflation-price-confusion-money-illusion.

16. **U.S. Bureau of Labor Statistics (BLS).** Monthly News Release: The Employment Situation. [Online] https://www.bls.gov/news.release/pdf/empsit.pdf.

17. **Federal Reserve Economic Data (FRED).** Federal Reserve Bank of St. Louis. [Online] https://fred.stlouisfed.org/.

18. **U.S. Bureau of Labor Statistics (BLS).** Unemployment Rate (UNRATE data series), retrieved from FRED, Federal Reserve Bank of St. Louis. [Online] https://fred.stlouisfed.org/series/UNRATE.

19. —. All Employees, Total Nonfarm (PAYEMS data series), retrieved from FRED, Federal Reserve Bank of St. Louis. [Online] https://fred.stlouisfed.org/series/PAYEMS.

20. **U.S. Bureau of Economic Analysis (BEA).** [Online] https://www.bea.gov/.

21. **National Bureau of Economic Research (NBER).** Business Cycle Dating. [Online] https://www.nber.org/research/business-cycle-dating.

22. **U.S. Bureau of Economic Analysis (BEA).** GDP: Gross Domestic Product. [Online] https://www.bea.gov/data/gdp/gross-domestic-product.

23. **McGlasson, Mary J.** (Macro) Episode 20: GDP (3:51). *mjmfoodie YouTube channel.* [Online]

REFERENCES

https://www.youtube.com/watch?v=yUiU_xRPwMc&list=PLF2A3693D8481F442&index=21.

24. —. (Macro) Episode 21: Real GDP (2:37). *mjmfoodie YouTube channel.* [Online] https://www.youtube.com/watch?v=29S7FzI7s7g&list=PLF2A3693D8481F442&index=22.

25. **Marginal Revolution University (MRU).** GDP: What is Gross Domestic Product (GDP)? (4:35) Instructor: Alex Tabarrok. [Online] https://mru.org/courses/principles-economics-macroeconomics/gross-domestic-product-definition-what-is-gdp.

26. —. GDP: Nominal vs. Real GDP (7:41). Instructor: Alex Tabarrok. [Online] https://mru.org/courses/principles-economics-macroeconomics/real-versus-nominal-gdp.

27. **Hilsenrath, John.** A different Take on the U.S. Economy: Maybe It Isn't Really Shrinking. *The Wall Street Journal.* August 29, 2022.

28. **U.S. Bureau of Economic Analysis (BEA).** Real Gross Domestic Product (GDPC1 data series), Real gross domestic income (A261RX1Q020SBEA data series), retrieved from FRED, Federal Reserve Bank of St. Louis. [Online] https://fred.stlouisfed.org/graph/?id=GDPC1,A261RX1Q020SBEA.

29. —. Real gross domestic product per capita (A939RX0Q048SBEA data series), retrieved from FRED, Federal Reserve Bank of St. Louis. [Online] https://fred.stlouisfed.org/series/A939RX0Q048SBEA.

30. **Caplan, Bryan D.** How Everyone Can Get Richer as Per-Capita Income Falls. *EconLib The Library of Economics and Liberty.* [Online] March 27, 2005. https://www.econlib.org/archives/2005/03/how_everyone_ca.html.

31. **U.S. Bureau of Economic Analysis (BEA).** Real Personal Consumption Expenditure (PCECC96 data series), Real Gross Private Domestic Investment (GPDIC1), Government Purchases (GCEC1 data series), Real Exports (EXPGSC1), Real imports (IMPGSC1), retrieved from FRED, Federal Reserve Bank of St. Louis. [Online] https://fred.stlouisfed.org/graph/?id=PCECC96,GPDIC1,GCEC1,EXPGSC1,IMPGSC1.

REFERENCES

32. —. NIPA Handbook: Concepts and Methods of the U.S. National Income and Product Accounts. [Online] https://www.bea.gov/resources/methodologies/nipa-handbook.

33. **U.S. Bureau of Labor Statistics (BLS).** Monthly News Release: Consumer Price Index. [Online] https://www.bls.gov/news.release/pdf/cpi.pdf.

34. —. Archived News Releases: Consumer Price Index. [Online] https://www.bls.gov/bls/news-release/cpi.htm.

35. —. Consumer Price Index for All Urban Consumers: All Items in U.S. City Average, Seasonally Adjusted (CPIAUCSL series), retrieved from FRED, Federal Reserve Bank of St. Louis. [Online] https://fred.stlouisfed.org/series/CPIAUCSL.

36. —. Consumer Price Index for All Urban Consumers: All Items in U.S. City Average, Not Seasonally Adjusted (CPIAUCSL series), retrieved from FRED, Federal Reserve Bank of St. Louis. [Online] https://fred.stlouisfed.org/series/CPIAUCNS.

37. **Arnold, Roger A., Arnold, Daniel R. and Arnold, David H.** *Macroeconomics.* 14e. s.l. : Cengage, 2023.

38. **Marginal Revolution University (MRU).** Business Cycle Theories: The Keynesians (8:04). Instructor: Tyler Cowen. [Online] https://mru.org/courses/principles-economics-macroeconomics/business-cycle-theories-keynesian.

39. **Press, Daniel.** How the Federal Government Created the Subprime Mortgage Crisis. *Foundation for Economic Education (FEE).* [Online] February 14, 2018. https://fee.org/articles/how-the-federal-government-created-the-subprime-mortgage-crisis/.

40. **U.S. Department of Labor (DOL).** History of Federal Minimum Wage Rates Under the Fair Labor Standards Act, 1938-2009. [Online] https://www.dol.gov/agencies/whd/minimum-wage/history/chart.

41. **Mulligan, Robert F.** Understanding the Covid-19 Recession. *American Institute for Economic Research (AIER).* [Online] https://www.aier.org/article/understanding-the-covid-19-recession/.

42. **Pisani, Joseph.** It's Taylor Swift's Economy, and We're All Living in It. *The Wall Street Journal.* July 23, 2023.

REFERENCES

43. **Barro, Robert J.** Keynesian Economics vs. Regular Economics. *The Wall Street Journal.* August 24, 2011.

44. **U.S. Bureau of Economic Analysis (BEA).** National GDP & Personal Income. [Online] https://www.bea.gov/itable/national-gdp-and-personal-income.

45. **Marginal Revolution University (MRU).** Fiscal Policy: Introduction (3:26). Instructor: Tyler Cowen. [Online] https://mru.org/courses/principles-economics-macroeconomics/intro-fiscal-policy.

46. —. Fiscal Policy: The Best-Case Scenario (3:37). Instructor: Tyler Cowen. [Online] https://mru.org/courses/principles-economics-macroeconomics/expansionary-fiscal-policy.

47. —. Fiscal Policy: The Limits of Fiscal Policy (7:05). Instructor: Alex Tabarrok. [Online] https://mru.org/courses/principles-economics-macroeconomics/fiscal-policy-limitations.

48. —. Fiscal Policy: The Dangers of Fiscal Policy (6:02). Instructor: Alex Tabarrok. [Online] https://mru.org/courses/principles-economics-macroeconomics/fiscal-policy-dangers.

49. —. Fiscal Policy: Fiscal Policy & Crowding Out (5:25). Instructor: Alex Tabarrok. [Online] https://mru.org/courses/principles-economics-macroeconomics/fiscal-policy-crowding-out.

50. **U.S. Bureau of Economic Analysis (BEA).** Navigating BEA interactive data. [Online] https://www.youtube.com/watch?v=x6CL0MiYgfM.

51. **Marginal Revolution University (MRU).** Principles of Economics: Macroeconomics. Fiscal Policy: The Dangers of Fiscal Policy. [Online] https://mru.org/courses/principles-economics-macroeconomics/fiscal-policy-dangers.

52. **Boudreaux, Don J.** Quotation of the Day. *Cafe Hayek.* [Online] June 19, 2022. https://cafehayek.com/2022/06/quotation-of-the-day-3928.html.

53. **Cochrane, John H.** On the 2% Inflation Target. *The Grumpy Economist.* [Online] July 27, 2023. https://johnhcochrane.blogspot.com/2023/07/on-2-inflation-target.html.

REFERENCES

54. **Levy, Mickey D.** The Post-Covid Spending Spree's Stealthy Economic Stimulus. *The Wall Street Journal.* July 20, 2023.

55. **WSJ Editorial Board.** Fitch Downgrades America. *The Wall Street Journal.* August 2, 2023.

56. **FitchRatings.** Fitch Downgrades the United States' Long-Term Ratings to 'AA+' from 'AAA'; Outlook Stable. [Online] August 1, 2023. https://www.fitchratings.com/research/sovereigns/fitch-downgrades-united-states-long-term-ratings-to-aa-from-aaa-outlook-stable-01-08-2023.

57. **FRED Blog.** [Online] https://fredblog.stlouisfed.org/.

58. **Silva, Andre C. and Zimmermann, Christian.** Savings are now more liquid and part of "M1 noney". [Online] May 20, 2021. https://fredblog.stlouisfed.org/2021/05/savings-are-now-more-liquid-and-part-of-m1-money/.

59. **U.S. Federal Reserve Board (FRB).** Currency Component of M1 (CURRSL series), Demand Deposits (DEMDEPSL series), Other (OCDSL series), M1 (M1SL series), M2 (M2SL series), retrieved from FRED, Federal Reserve Bank of St. Louis. [Online] https://fred.stlouisfed.org/graph/?g=Ulfc.

60. **Marginal Revolution University (MRU).** Savings, Investment, & the Financial System: What Do Banks Do? (4:31). Instructor: Alex Tabarrok. [Online] https://mru.org/courses/principles-economics-macroeconomics/banks-financial-intermediaries.

61. —. Savings, Investment, & the Financial System: Intro to the Bond Market (6:23). Instructor: Alex Tabarrok. [Online]

62. **U.S. Federal Reserve Board (FRB).** M2 (M2SL series), retrieved from FRED, Federal Reserve Bank of St. Louis. [Online] https://fred.stlouisfed.org/series/M2SL.

63. **Cochrane, John H.** Inflation and the Value of Money. *The Grumpy Economist.* [Online] March 17, 2024. https://www.grumpy-economist.com/p/inflation-and-the-value-of-money.

64. **National Bureau of Economic Research (NBER).** [Online] https://www.nber.org/.

REFERENCES

65. **Bolhuis, Marijin A., et al.** The Cost of Money is Part of the Cost of Living: New Evidence on the Consumer Sentiment Anomaly. *National Bureau of Economic Research (NBER) Working Papers.* [Online] February 2024. https://www.nber.org/papers/w32163.

66. **U.S. Federal Reserve Board (FRB).** About the Fed. [Online] https://www.federalreserve.gov/aboutthefed.htm.

67. —. Monetary Policy. [Online] https://www.federalreserve.gov/monetarypolicy.htm.

68. **U.S. Congress.** House Bill 2543 - Federal Reserve Racial and Economic Equity Act. [Online] https://www.congress.gov/bill/117th-congress/house-bill/2543.

69. **WSJ Editorial Board.** A Woke Mandate for the Federal Reserve. *The Wall Street Journal.* June 21, 2022.

70. **U.S. Senate.** Senate Bill 1327 - Federal Reserve Racial and Economic Equity Act. [Online] https://www.congress.gov/bill/117th-congress/senate-bill/1327.

71. —. Senate Bill 2257 - Federal Racial and Economic Equity Act. [Online] https://www.congress.gov/bill/118th-congress/senate-bill/2257.

72. **U.S. Federal Reserve Board (FRB).** Press Release: Federal Reserve Board invites public comment on proposed principles providing a high-level framework for the safe and sound management of exposures to climate-related financial risks for large banking organizations. [Online] December 2, 2022. https://www.federalreserve.gov/newsevents/pressreleases/other20221202b.htm.

73. —. Principles for Climate-Related Financial Risk Management for Large Financial Institutions. *Federal Register.* [Online] December 8, 2022. https://www.federalregister.gov/documents/2022/12/08/2022-26648/principles-for-climate-related-financial-risk-management-for-large-financial-institutions.

74. **Waller, J. Christopher.** Statement by Governor Waller on principles for climate-related financial risk management for large financial institutions. *U.S. Federal Reserve Board (FRB).* [Online] December 2, 2022. https://www.federalreserve.gov/newsevents/pressreleases/waller-statement-20221202.htm.

REFERENCES

75. **Powell, Jerome H.** Live speech. International Symposium on Central Bank Independence, Stockholm, Sweden. Panel 3: Central Bank independence and the mandate: Evolving views (30:05-34:44). *Sveriges Riksbank.* [Online] January 10, 2023. https://www.riksbank.se/en-gb/press-and-published/conferences/2023/international-symposium-on-central-bank-independence/.

76. **Sveriges Riksbank (Sweden's central bank).** [Online] https://www.riksbank.se/en-gb.

77. **Powell, Jerome H.** Prepared speech. Sveriges Riksbank (Sweden's central bank): International Symposium on Central Bank Independence. Panel 3: Central Bank Independence and the Mandate-Evolving Views. *The Federal Reserve.* [Online] January 10, 2023. https://www.federalreserve.gov/newsevents/speech/powell20230110a.htm.

78. **Cochrane, John H.** Cheers for Powell. *The Grumpy Economist.* [Online] January 10, 2023. https://johnhcochrane.blogspot.com/2023/01/cheers-for-powell.html.

79. **U.S. Bureau of Economic Analysis (BEA).** Gross Domestic Product (GDP data series), Real Gross Domestic Product (GDPC1 data series), retrieved from FRED, Federal Reserve Bank of St. Louis. [Online] https://fred.stlouisfed.org/graph/?id=GDP,GDPC1,.

80. **Marginal Revolution University (MRU).** Inflation & Quantity Theory of Money: Quantity Theory of Money (3:27). Instructor: Alex Tabarrok. [Online]

81. **Ip, Greg.** Inflation Surge Earns Monetarism Another Look. *The Wall Street Journal.* June 22, 2022.

82. **Hilsenrath, Jon.** Janet Yellen's Learning Curve. *The Wall Street Journal.* October 21, 2022.

83. **Mackintosh, James.** Monetarism Is Back. It May Not Last. *The Wall Street Journal.* October 6, 2023.

84. **Steinhauser, Gabriele.** Zimbabwe Launches a New Currency ... Again. *The Wall Street Journal.* April 5, 2024.

85. **Marginal Revolution Univesity (MRU).** Monetary Policy & the Federal Reserve: Monetary Policy & the Fed. Instructor: Alex Tabarrok. [Online]

REFERENCES

https://mru.org/courses/principles-economics-macroeconomics/monetary-policy-federal-reserve-system.

86. **Luther, William J. and Salter, Alexander W.** Lessons for Today From the Gold Standard. *The Wall Street Journal.* August 2, 2021.

87. **U.S. Federal Reserve Board (FRB).** Federal Open Market Committee (FOMC). [Online] https://www.federalreserve.gov/monetarypolicy/fomc.htm.

88. —. Press Release: Federal Reserve issues FOMC statement. [Online] November 2, 2022. https://www.federalreserve.gov/newsevents/pressreleases/monetary20221102 a.htm.

89. **Powell, Jerome H.** FOMC Press Conference: Transcript of Chair Powell's Press Conference. [Online] November 2, 2022. https://www.federalreserve.gov/mediacenter/files/FOMCpresconf20221102.pd f.

90. **Shelton, Judy.** The Fed's Monetary Policy Tool Kit Needs an Overhaul. *The Wall Street Journal.* June 13, 2023.

91. **Congressional Budget Office (CBO).** An Update to the Budget and Economic Outlook: 2021 to 2031. [Online] July 2021. https://www.cbo.gov/system/files/2021-07/57218-Outlook.pdf.

92. **Congresssional Budget Office (CBO).** How the Fiscal Responsibility Act of 2023 Affects CBO's Projections of Federal Debt. [Online] June 2023. https://www.cbo.gov/system/files/2023-06/59235-Debt.pdf.

93. **U.S. Federal Reserve Board (FRB).** [Online] https://www.youtube.com/@federalreserve.

94. —. FOMC Press Conferences playlist. *federalreserve YouTube channel.* [Online] https://www.youtube.com/playlist?list=PL159CD41EB36CFE86.

95. **Timiraos, Nick.** Powell Says Fed Must Accept Higher Recession Risk to Combat Inflation. *The Wall Street Journal.* June 29, 2022.

96. —. Why Consumers' Inflation Psychology Is Stoking Anxiety at the Fed. *The Wall Street Journal.* July 5, 2022.

REFERENCES

97. **Cochrane, John H.** Inflation Expectations. *The Grumpy Economist.* [Online] October 25, 2022. https://johnhcochrane.blogspot.com/2022/10/inflation-expectations.html.

98. **Sternberg, Joseph C.** Why Is the Federal Reserve Always Surprised by Inflation? *The Wall Street Journal.* April 18, 2024.

99. **U.S. Federal Reserve Board (FRB).** FRB/US: Federal Reserve Board Model of the U.S. Economy. [Online] https://www.federalreserve.gov/econres/us-models-about.htm.

100. **University of Michigan, Institute for Social Research (ISR) Survey Research Center (SRC).** [Online] https://src.isr.umich.edu/.

101. **—.** Surveys of Consumers Attitudes (SCA) Project Website. [Online] http://www.sca.isr.umich.edu/.

102. **—.** Economic Behavior Research. [Online] https://src.isr.umich.edu/research-themes/economic-behavior.

103. **—.** Surveys of Consumers Attitudes (SCA) Data Site, Reports. [Online] https://data.sca.isr.umich.edu/reports.php.

104. **Cochrane, John H.** Truss Tragedy. *The Grumpy Economist.* [Online] October 25, 2022. https://johnhcochrane.blogspot.com/2022/10/truss-tragedy.html.

105. **Hubbard, R. Glenn.** Put Growth Back on the Political Agenda. *The Wall Street Journal.* April 18, 2024.

106. **Heaton, Andrew and Sarah Rose Siskind.** Mostly Weekly Series Finale: Creative Destruction. [Online] https://www.youtube.com/watch?v=132XUomFEEs.

107. **Boudreaux, Don J.** Some Links. *Cafe Hayek.* [Online] July 19, 2022. https://cafehayek.com/2022/07/some-links-1753.html.

108. **WSJ Editorial Board.** Congress Goes All in for Computer Chip Subsidies. *The Wall Street Journal.* July 19, 2022.

109. **U.S. Congress.** House Bill 4346 - Chips and Science Act. [Online] https://www.congress.gov/bill/117th-congress/house-bill/4346.

REFERENCES

110. **WSJ Editorial Board.** Intel and Industrial Policy in Action. *The Wall Street Journal.* April 3, 2024.

111. **Hannon, Paul.** ECB Must Narrow Interest-Rate Gap With Fed, OECD Says. *The Wall Street Journal.* November 22, 2022.

112. **Organisation for Econonomic Co-operation & Development (OECD).** [Online] https://www.oecd.org/.

113. **European Central Bank (ECB).** [Online] https://www.ecb.europa.eu/home/html/index.en.html.

114. **Boudreaux, Don J.** Debunking Yet Another False Tale Told About American Trade Deficits. *Cafe Hayek.* [Online] April 16, 2023. https://cafehayek.com/2023/04/debunking-yet-another-false-tale-told-about-american-trade-deficits.html.

115. —. Griswold and Freytag On the So-Called "Trade Deficit". *Cafe Hayek.* [Online] April 25, 2023. https://cafehayek.com/2023/04/griswold-and-freytag-on-the-so-called-trade-deficit.html.

INDEX

INDEX

CHARTS LIST

www.ingramcontent.com/pod-product-compliance
Lightning Source LLC
Chambersburg PA
CBHW071956210526
45479CB00003B/962